THE MANDALORIAN

Music by
LUDWIG GÖRANSSON

Piano Solo

STAR WARS
THE
MANDALORIAN

Music from the Disney+ Original Series

MUSIC BY
LUDWIG GÖRANSSON

© 2020 & TM Lucasfilm Ltd. All Rights Reserved

ISBN 978-1-5400-9034-8

HAL•LEONARD®

Visit Hal Leonard Online at
www.halleonard.com

Contact us:
Hal Leonard
7777 West Bluemound Road
Milwaukee, WI 53213
Email: info@halleonard.com

In Europe, contact:
Hal Leonard Europe Limited
42 Wigmore Street
Marylebone, London, W1U 2RN
Email: info@halleonardeurope.com

In Australia, contact:
Hal Leonard Australia Pty. Ltd.
4 Lentara Court
Cheltenham, Victoria, 3192 Australia
Email: info@halleonard.com.au

Contents

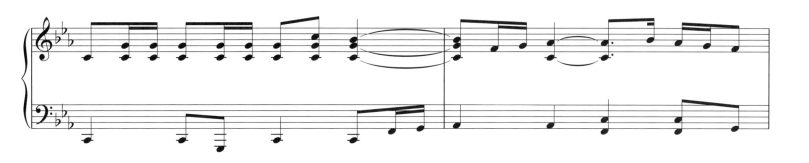

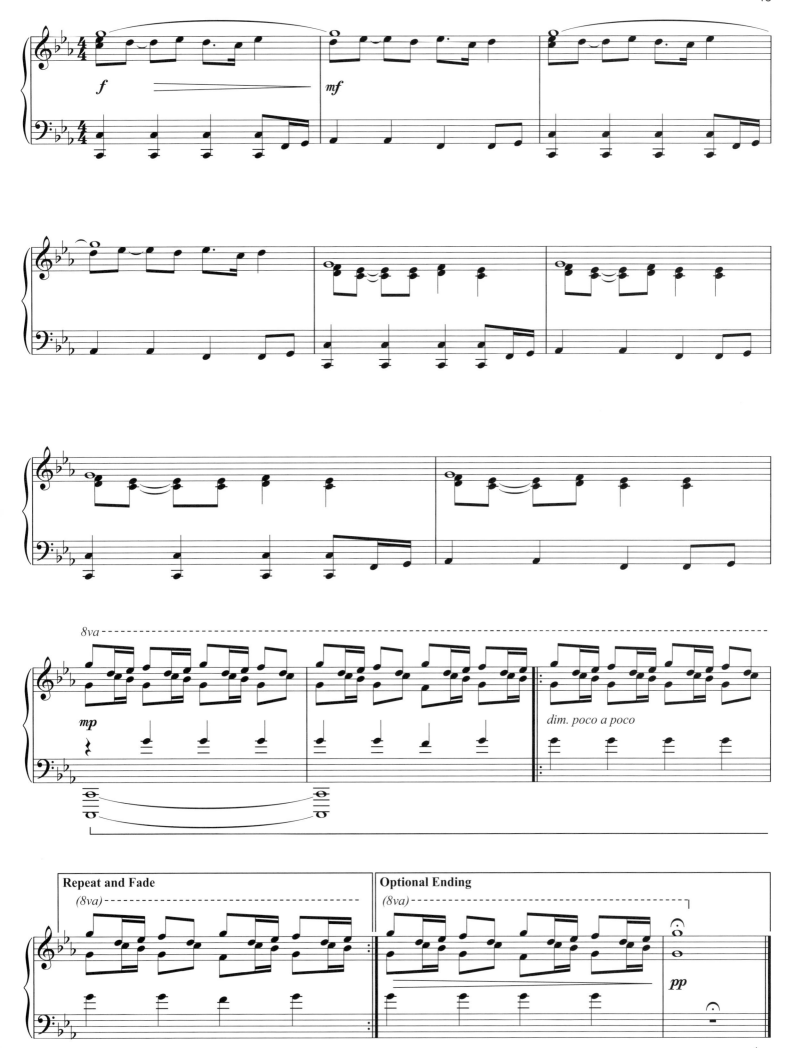

TO THE JAWAS

Music by
LUDWIG GÖRANSSON

SIGNET FORGING

Music by
LUDWIG GÖRANSSON

Ominous

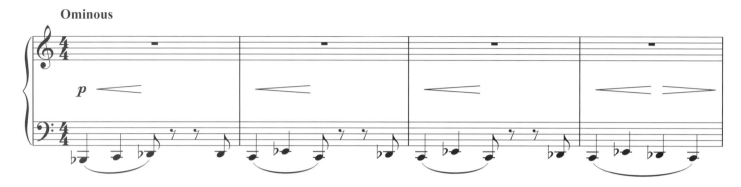

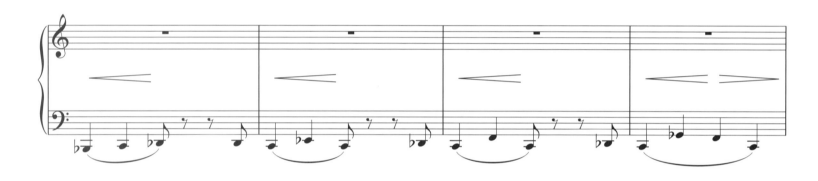

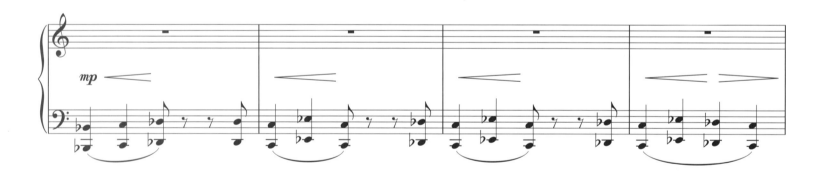

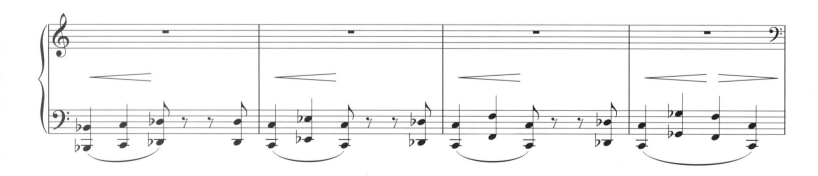

I NEED ONE OF THOSE

Music by
LUDWIG GÖRANSSON

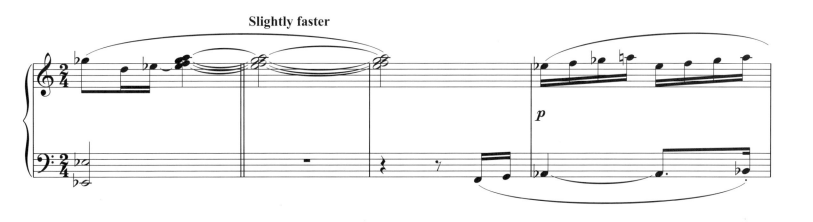

Stately

MANDO RESCUE

Music by
LUDWIG GÖRANSSON

THE PONDS OF SORGAN

Music by
LUDWIG GÖRANSSON

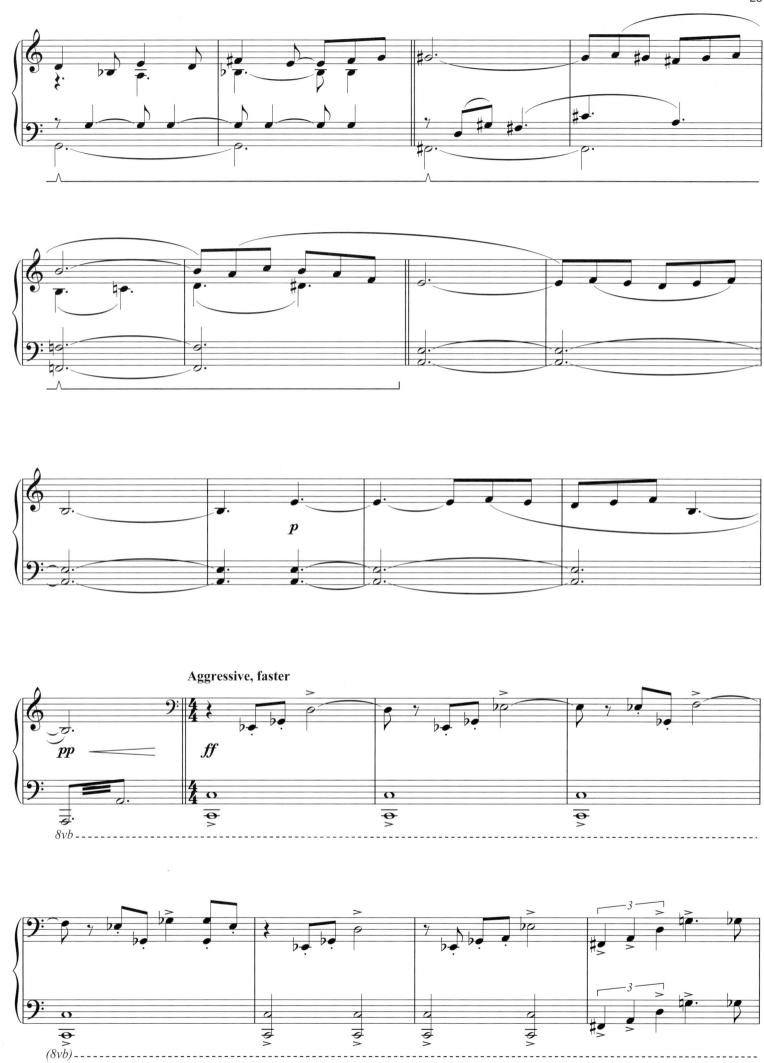

CAN I FEED HIM?

Music by
LUDWIG GÖRANSSON

FAREWELL

Music by
LUDWIG GÖRANSSON

BRIGHT EYES

Music by
LUDWIG GÖRANSSON

Delicate

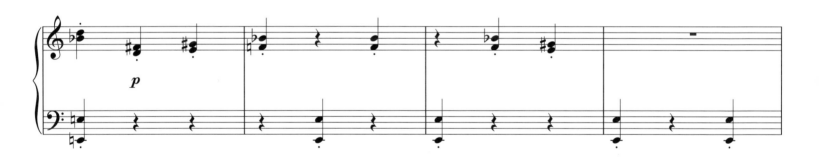

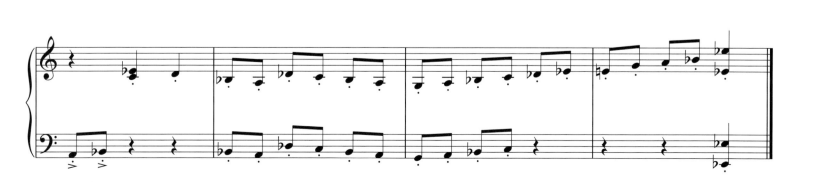

SPEEDERBIKES

Music by
LUDWIG GÖRANSSON

THIS IS IT

Music by
LUDWIG GÖRANSSON

THE EWEBB

Music by
LUDWIG GÖRANSSON

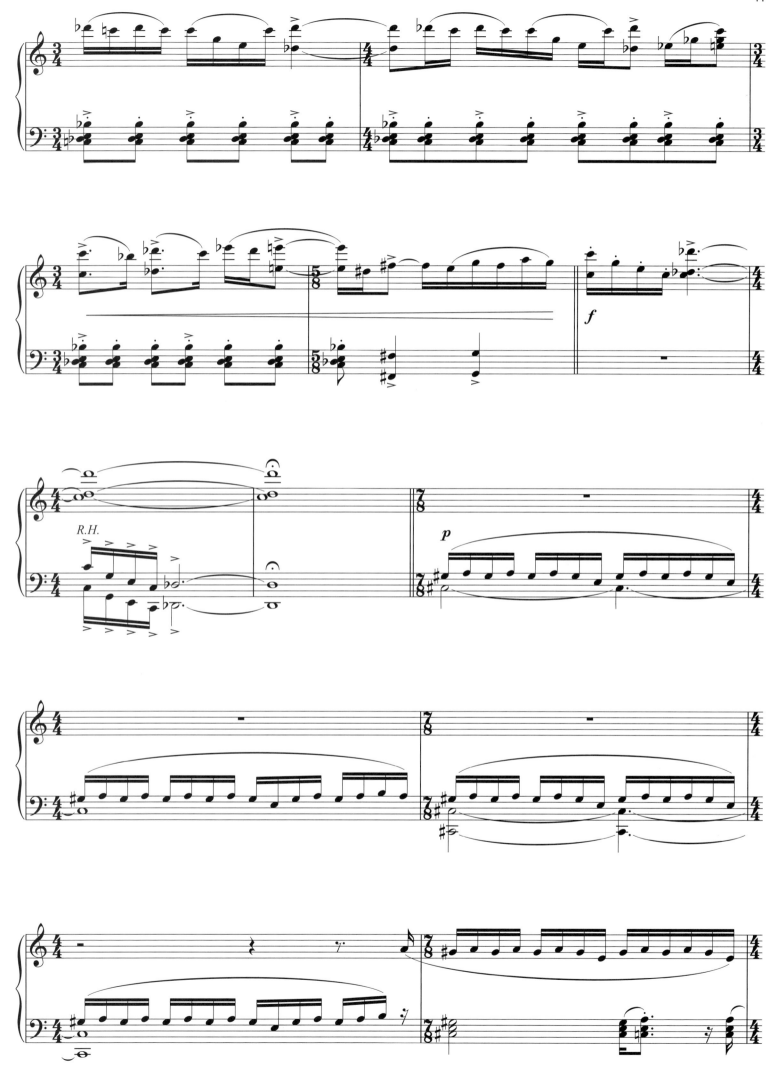

SACRIFICE

Music by
LUDWIG GÖRANSSON

A WARRIOR'S DEATH

Music by
LUDWIG GÖRANSSON

Dramatic!

THE BABY

Music by
LUDWIG GÖRANSSON

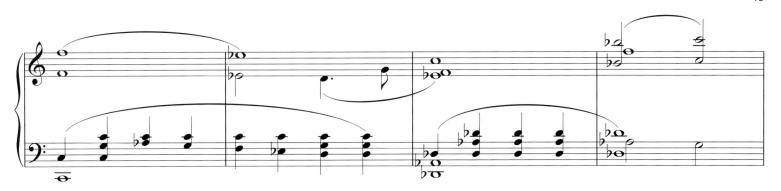

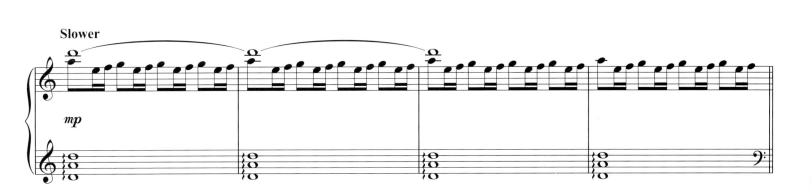

THE MANDALORIAN
(Orchestral Version)

Music by
LUDWIG GÖRANSSON

Dramatically